I am a

GREEK
ORTHODOX

# I am a GREEK ORTHODOX

**Maria Roussou**
meets
**Panos Papamichael**

**Photography: Chris Fairclough**

Religious Consultant:
Archbishop Methodios of
Thyateira and Great Britain

**WATTS BOOKS**
LONDON • NEW YORK • SYDNEY

Panos Papamichael is eleven years
old. His father, Demos Papamichael,
is a shopkeeper. His mother, Andri
Papamichael looks after the house
and helps in the shop. Panos's older
brother Michael is thirteen years old.
His sister Marina is seven. Panos goes
to a comprehensive school in Enfield,
London.

# Contents

© 1985 Watts Books

Watts Books
96 Leonard Street
London
EC2A 4RH

Franklin Watts Australia
14 Mars Road
Lane Cove
NSW 2066

ISBN 0 86313 259 6 (hardback)
ISBN 0 7496 1409 9 (paperback)

Paperback edition 1993

The Publishers would like to thank the Papamichael family and the congregations of St Sophia's Cathedral, St Barnabas Wood Green and All Saints' Church, Camden.

10 9 8 7 6 5 4 3 2 1

Printed in Italy

## The Greek Orthodox Belief

**We are Greek Orthodox Christians. My mother keeps an album of the family and church events.**

The Christian faith has three main branches – Orthodox, Roman Catholic and Protestant Churches. The Orthodox Church is the continuation of the first Church founded by Christ and his Apostles. The Church keeps the original teachings and is organized according to apostolic practice. Orthodox means "correctly believing".

**The Archbishop tells us to worship God and show great respect to Mary and the Saints.**

Orthdox Christians, like all Christians, believe in Jesus Christ as Lord, God and Saviour. They deeply respect the Virgin Mary, the Mother of God whom they call Theotokos, the one who gave birth to Jesus Christ. By praying to the Virgin Mary and the Saints, Orthodox people believe that they communicate with God. Orthodox churches are decorated with icons and wall paintings of Jesus Christ, Mary and the saints.

## Going to church

**On Sunday morning we always go to church. Sometimes we go to St Sophia's Cathedral. We each light a candle when we go inside.**

Greek Orthodox churches are found in areas where there is a large Greek community. All churches are named after a saint or an event in the Life of Christ. The local church for the Papamichael family is St Barnabas in London. When Greek Orthodox people enter a church they make the sign of the Cross, donate money and take a candle to light.

Our churches are very beautiful inside. We must kiss the icons before the service begins.

When icons are kissed, a person is showing their love and respect for the people shown in the icons. It is hoped that these people will pray to God for the person. The church is divided into two parts by the icon screen. The congregation sings and prays in front of the screen. Behind the screen is the Altar and only priests can go there. Big churches have choirs to sing the hymns.

## The Sunday Service

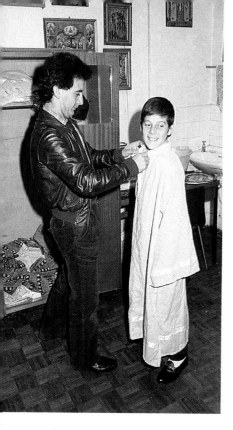

**I wear special robes when I help the priest during a service or other ceremonies. I sometimes carry a candle or hold the incense.**

The service, called the Divine Liturgy, has been very much the same since the first centuries after Christ. There are hymns, readings from the Bible and special prayers. The smell of burning incense and the melody of the hymns is said to express thanks to God.

**I listen carefully to what the priests say. They are wise men and help me to understand the words of God found in the Bible.**

The priest explains Bible readings, in a sermon, by examples from everyday life. The priests play an important part in the life of any Greek community. Priests can be married but Bishops, Archbishops and the Patriarchs must be single. Each parish has a church committee which help the priests in the Church and in activities in the community.

**During the Sunday Service the priest talks to us in front of the Altar. He explains the Bible and other things about our religion.**

The Greek Orthodox Bible is written in the ancient Greek language used by the Apostles except for the Gospel of St. Matthew which is in Aramaic. The priest explains about the history of Christianity and the lives of the saints. Children are taught to recite a special prayer called the Creed which begins: 'I believe in One God . . .'. Hymns for different feast days are also learned. The Priest talks about the icons and the meaning of the Cross.

# Holy Communion

**At the end of the service, I take Holy Communion. The priest gives me the wine and bread.**

The Holy Communion is the most sacred event during the Sunday Service. Orthodox people believe that they receive Christ Himself in the wine and bread. The wine is His Blood and the Bread His Body. Many people do not eat meat for some days before Holy Communion and make a special effort to love each other.

| The Greek Script |
|---|
| Α Β Γ Δ Ε Ζ |
| Η Θ Ι Κ Λ Μ |
| Ν Ξ Ο Π Ρ Σ |
| Τ Υ Φ Χ Ψ Ω |

## Greek classes

**I go to classes every week to learn the Greek language. This will help me to know more about my faith.**

Greek people usually want their children to learn about their homeland. Most Greek Orthodox churches and Greek Priest's Associations offer lessons to children. They can learn to speak, read and write the Greek language. This will also help them to understand the Church services held in Greek.

**We also read stories about Greece and Cyprus. But what I like best is the Greek dancing.**

The children learn about the long history of Greece and Cyprus and their peoples. They are given Greek books to read. As most people in Panos's Church come from Cyprus they learn about the special customs and history of the island of Cyprus. There are many types of Greek dances – some very old and some modern. Greek songs are also taught to the children.

# The history of Panos's family

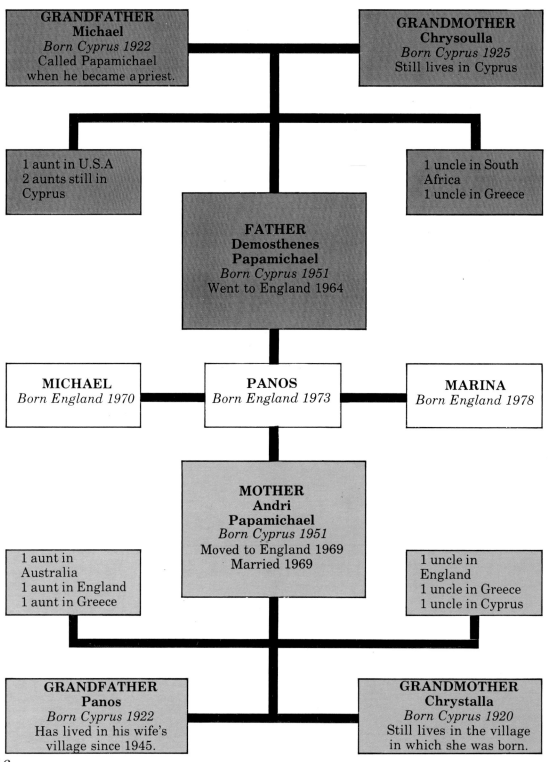

**GRANDFATHER**
**Michael**
*Born Cyprus 1922*
Called Papamichael
when he became a priest.

**GRANDMOTHER**
**Chrysoulla**
*Born Cyprus 1925*
Still lives in Cyprus

1 aunt in U.S.A
2 aunts still in
Cyprus

1 uncle in South
Africa
1 uncle in Greece

**FATHER**
**Demosthenes**
**Papamichael**
*Born Cyprus 1951*
Went to England 1964

**MICHAEL**
*Born England 1970*

**PANOS**
*Born England 1973*

**MARINA**
*Born England 1978*

**MOTHER**
**Andri**
**Papamichael**
*Born Cyprus 1951*
Moved to England 1969
Married 1969

1 aunt in
Australia
1 aunt in England
1 aunt in Greece

1 uncle in
England
1 uncle in Greece
1 uncle in Cyprus

**GRANDFATHER**
**Panos**
*Born Cyprus 1922*
Has lived in his wife's
village since 1945.

**GRANDMOTHER**
**Chrystalla**
*Born Cyprus 1920*
Still lives in the village
in which she was born.

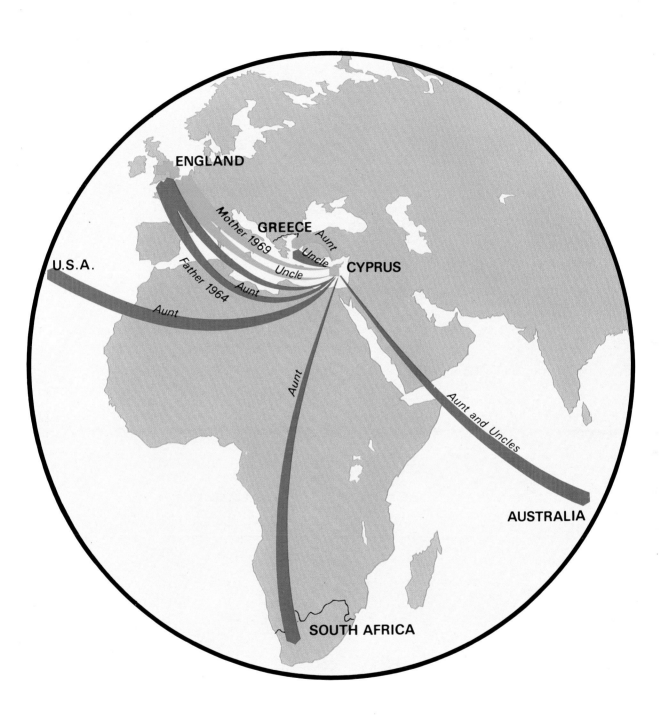

ENGLAND

GREECE

Mother 1969

Aunt

Uncle

U.S.A.

Father 1964

Uncle

Aunt

CYPRUS

Aunt

Aunt

Aunt and Uncles

AUSTRALIA

SOUTH AFRICA

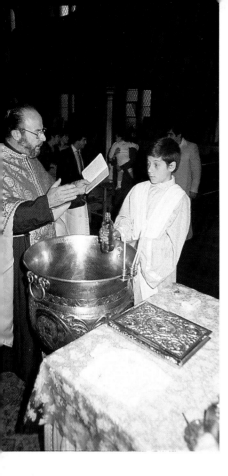

# Baptism

**I often help the priest in the baptism of babies. Special oil is poured into the water.**

Baptism is an important ceremony in the Orthodox Church. At baptism the child becomes a member of the Church. The baby is dipped three times in the water containing the baptismal oil in the name of the Holy Trinity – the Father, the Son and the Holy Spirit. The child is then given its Christian name by its godparents. Usually it is the name of a grandparent or a special saint.

**Then the priest gives the baby to the godparent and puts another special oil on its head.**

The godparent is given the baby in a white unwashed piece of cloth. The priest makes the sign of the Cross on its forehead with a holy oil called Chrism. After this he says: "The seal of the gift of the Holy Spirit." The priest then cuts three pieces of hair from the baby's head as a sign that its life is dedicated to Christ. The baby and a candle are then given to the mother.

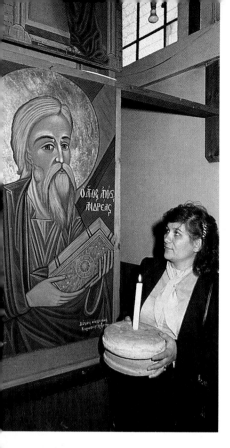

## Name Days

**On our Name Days we go to the Church for a special ceremony.**

The Christian name given to a Greek Orthodox person is celebrated each year on the feast day of the Saint of that name. Christian names are those named after Christ, Mary, the Apostles of Christ, Church Fathers and the Saints. Panos's mother is called Andri, the female of St Andrew. On her Name Day she brings offerings to the Church and has Holy Communion.

**Bread, or "artos" is put on a table with kolliva and candles. We eat the food afterwards.**

The things brought to the Church, apart from bread, kolliva (boiled wheat) and candles, are oil and wine. Everybody in the Church is given a candle which is lit during the service. The name Panos is linked to that of Mary, the Mother of Christ, who is called Panayia—"Most Holy." Marina, his sister, is named after St Marina, the patron of her mother's village in Cyprus. Michael is named after the Archangel Michael.

## Greek weddings

**I like going to engagements and weddings as there are always parties afterwards.**

When Greek people decide to get married an engagement ceremony is held. During the ceremony the couple exchange rings as a sign of their love and devotion to each other. The priest gives them a blessing and their families get to know each other. At the wedding the bride and groom are led into the Church by their fathers.

**The priest holds a silver crown, called a "Stefana" over the heads of the people being married.**

The wedding ceremony takes place in front of the Altar and the Icon Screen. The choir sings hymns and readings are made from the Bible. The priest takes the hands of the couplē. He joins them together for life by blessing their rings and their crowns. After the wedding the guests give their wishes to the couple. Special almond sweets from a decorated basket are eaten. Then there is a big feast.

## Christmas and New Year

I look forward to our festivals. We have a big meal after Church on Christmas Day and make a St Basil's cake on New Year's Eve.

Christmas is celebrated on 25th December in much the same way as other Christian Churches. Hymns and carols are sung in the Church. On New Year's Eve every family makes a cake with a special coin in it. St Basil was a bishop in the fourth century after Christ. The person who gets the coin is said to be lucky for the next year.

## Lent

During Lent we remember Christ's fast in the desert. We do not eat meat at the meal on the first day of Lent.

The first day of Lent, in February or early March, is called "Clean Monday" because no meat or other animal products can be eaten. A special meal is prepared on this day to celebrate the beginning of Lent. The forty days of Lent are a time of family prayer and fasting which end at Easter.

## Easter

**We all go to Church on the night before Easter Sunday. We go home to light candles with the Holy Light and have a meal.**

The Resurrection, Christ's rising from the dead, is celebrated on Easter Night. Churches are kept in darkness until the priest opens the doors of the Altar. He comes out with a candle announcing that Christ is risen. From this candle everyone lights a candle. Special prayers are said before eating.

**I enjoy cracking the red Easter eggs at the Easter night meal.**

The red-dyed eggs stand for the victory of the new life of Christ over death. Easter is a very happy time with special foods. It is the end of the fast for Lent and also celebrates the end of winter. There are also games and dancing in which people of all ages take part. Children get their new summer clothes as Easter presents. The festival of Easter lasts for 40 days until the feast of Christ's Ascension into Heaven.

# The Orthodox Year

Most Orthodox Churches, including the Greek, use the normal calendar. Some, such as the Russian and Serbian Churches, follow the Old Calendar which is 13 days behind. There are festivals during all seasons of the year.

DECEMBER

NOVEMBER

OCTOBER

SEPTEMBER

AUGUST

JULY

**CHRISTMAS**
*25th December*
Celebrates the birth of Jesus Christ.

**ST. ANDREW'S DAY**
*30th November*
A Name Day

**THE HOLY DAY OF ARCHANGEL MICHAEL**
*8th November*
A Name Day

**ST. DEMETRIUS'S DAY**
*26th October*
A Name Day

**ASSUMPTION**
*15th August*
Remembers the reception of Mary, the Mother of God, into Heaven.

**ST. MARINA'S DAY**
*17th July*
A Name Day

## St BASIL'S DAY

*1st January*

Celebrates St Basil, a bishop in the 4th Century AD. A special cake containing a silver coin is made and eaten.

### BAPTISM OF CHRIST

*6th January*

Water is blessed and bottles of Holy water taken home. Crosses are thrown into the sea and people compete to rescue them. Children baptise oranges.

## LENT

*February/March/April*

Remembers Christ's fast in the desert. Begins on 'Clean Monday' with a special meal and ends at Easter. It is a time of family prayer and fasting. The exact time of Lent is determined by the date of Good Friday which is the Friday following the first full moon after the Spring Equinox.

## EASTER

*April/May 40 days*

The most important feast of the year which celebrates the Resurrection of Christ. A time of great joy with special meals and activities. Also a celebration of the end of Winter.

## ASCENSION

*May/June 1 day*

Celebrates the return of Christ to Heaven and is the end of the Easter Festival.

# Facts and Figures

There are about 9½ million Greek Orthodox Christians in the world. The large majority are found in Greece and Cyprus where Greek Orthodoxy is the state religion.

About 200,000 Greek Orthodox live in Britain. Other large Greek Orthodox communities live in the United States, Australia, Germany and South America.

The Orthodox Church has branches in many countries including Russia, Romania and Bulgaria.

The different branches of the Orthodox Church in the world are thought to have a total membership of 150 million members. The Russian Orthodox Church is estimated to have 40–50 million. There are about 3½ million Orthodox people in North America.

The Catholic Church has about 700 million members and the total Christian church over 1,000 million.
The Patriarch of Constantinople, Turkey, is the head of the Greek Orthodox Churches outside Greece. He is based at Istanbul (the modern name for Constantinople) in Turkey. He is also seen as the "first" bishop of the complete Orthodox Church.

Responsible to the Patriarch of Constantinople are Archbishops found in different countries. In Britain there is the Archbishop of Thyateira and Great Britain. In North America there is the Archbishop of New York and North America.

The Orthodox Church follow the earliest traditions of the Christian Church begun by the Apostles of Jesus.

The Order of Service, or Divine Liturgy, held today by the Greek Orthodox Church, is named after St John Chrysostom, a Patriarch of Constantinople in the 4th Century AD. It was first written in Greek but has been translated into many other languages.

In recent years the Orthodox Church has worked towards co-operation with other Christian Churches. The Greek Orthodox Church is a member of the World Council of Churches. There have been several meetings between the Patriarch of Constantinople and the Pope. The latest meeting was in 1979 when Pope John Paul II visited Turkey.

# Glossary

**Baptism** The ceremony when a child is given its Christian name and received into the Church.

**Bible** The Christian Holy Book. It is divided into two parts. The Old Testament was written in early Jewish times and is also the Jewish Holy Book. The New Testament continues the life and works of Jesus Christ.

**Cross** The symbol of Christianity. Jesus Christ was nailed to a wooden cross, or crucifix, and left to die.

**Divine Liturgy** The service of Holy Communion in a Greek Orthodox Church, which has remained the same since the early days of Christianity.

**Easter** The festival to remember the death and rising from the dead of Jesus Christ.

**Holy Communion** The ceremony which remembers the last meal of Christ at which Christians receive the Body of Christ. Bread and wine are said to become the Body and Blood of Christ.

**Icons** Paintings of Christ, Mary, the Mother of Christ and saints in Orthodox Churches.

**Icon Screen** The wooden Barrier between the Holy Altar and the main part of the Church where the congregation sits.

**Incense** A spice which gives off a sweet smell when burned.

**Lent** The time of fasting before Easter which remembers the 40 day fast of Christ in the desert.

**Patriarch** The leading bishop in an Orthodox Christian Church.

**Resurrection** The arising of Christ from the dead.

**Saints** Holy men and women held in very high regard through their special lives and deeds. Orthodox Christians believe they reveal something about the holiness of God.

**Sacraments** Christian ceremonies which are said to be signs of God's grace towards those receiving them. The Sacraments include Baptism, Confirmation, Ordination of priests, Holy Communion and Marriage.

# Index